A Note to Parents and Teachers

DK READERS is a compelling reading programme for children, designed in conjunction with leading literacy experts, including Cliff Moon M.Ed., Honorary Fellow of the University of Reading. Cliff Moon has spent many years as a teacher and teacher educator specializing in reading and has written more than 140 books for children and teachers. He reviews regularly for teachers' journals.

Beautiful illustrations and superb full-colour photographs combine with engaging, easy-to-read stories to offer a fresh approach to each subject in the series. Each DK READER is guaranteed to capture a child's interest while developing his or her reading skills, general knowledge, and love of reading.

The five levels of DK READERS are aimed at different reading abilities, enabling you to choose the books that are exactly right for your child:

Pre-level 1: Learning to read
Level 1: Beginning to read
Level 2: Beginning to read alone
Level 3: Reading alone
Level 4: Proficient readers

The "normal" age at which a child begins to read can be anywhere from three to eight years old, so these levels are only a general guideline.

No matter which level you select, you can be sure that you are helping your child learn to read, then read to learn!

DK

LONDON, NEW YORK, MUNICH,
MELBOURNE AND DELHI

Series Editor Deborah Lock
Designer Sadie Thomas
Production Alison Lenane
DTP Designer Almudena Díaz
and Pilar Morales
Jacket Designer Simon Oon

Reading Consultant
Cliff Moon, M.Ed.

Published in Great Britian by Dorling Kindersley Limited
80, Strand, London WC2R ORL
6 8 10 9 7 5

A Penguin Company

A CIP record for this book is available
from the British Library

ISBN 978-1-4053-0602-7

Colour reproduction by Colourscan, Singapore
Printed and bound in China by L Rex Printing Co., Ltd.

The publisher would like to thank the following for their kind
permission to reproduce their photographs:
a=above; c=centre; b=below; l=left; r=right t=top;

www.agripicture.com: Peter Dean 22–23. **Alamy Images:** Bildagentur
Geduldig/archivberlin Fotoagentur GmbH 18-19; Jack Sullivan 26-27.
Ardea.com: John Daniels 10-11. **Corbis:** Darrell Gulin 8-9; Kit Houghton
24-25; Randy M. Ury 4-5. **DK Picture Library:** Barleylands Farm Museum
and Animal Centre 6, 8–9, 16; Philip Dowell 12, 14, 15, 18; Jerry Young
15; Tracy Morgan 15; Odds Farm Park 19; Barrie Watts 20, 21.
Getty Images: Pal Hermansen 20t; Hans Reinhard 11t. **Holt Studios
International:** 15t. **Oxford Scientific Films:** Mark Hamblin 14-15;
Konrad Wothe 12t.

All other images © Dorling Kindersley
For further information see: www.dkimages.com

DK READERS

LEARNING
pre-level
1
TO READ

Farm
Animals

A Dorling Kindersley Book

Come and meet
my friends
on the farm.

farmhouse

barn

5

feathers

chickens

Here is the chicken
with her little chicks.

chick

Here is a turkey coming to meet you.

beak

 turkeys

feathers

Here is the pig and here are the three pink piglets.

piglet

pigs

ear

Here are the cows
looking at you.

hoof

COWS

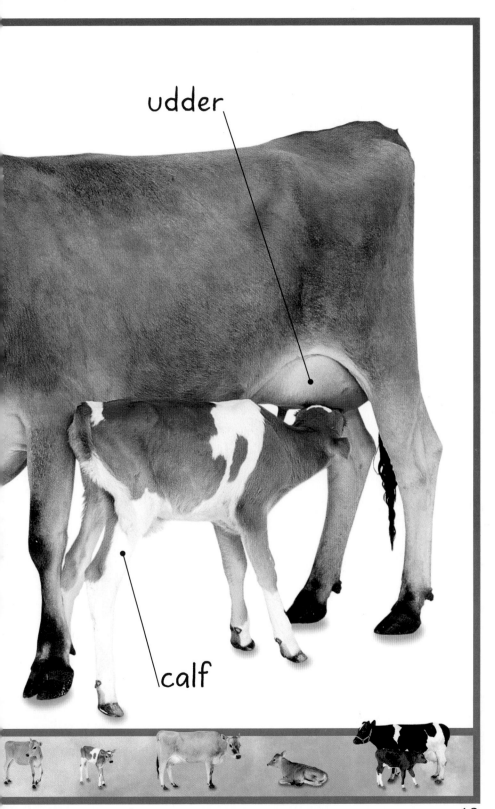

udder

calf

13

Here is a dog and here are her three sleepy puppies.

nose

puppy

dogs

Here is a sheep with her little lambs.

lamb

sheep

wool

ear

17

nose

goats

Here is a goat
lying down
with her kid.

kid

Here are the ducks
with their
fluffy ducklings.

 ducks

beak

duckling

21

Here are the geese
looking all around.

 geese

eye

neck

Here is a horse running with her foal.

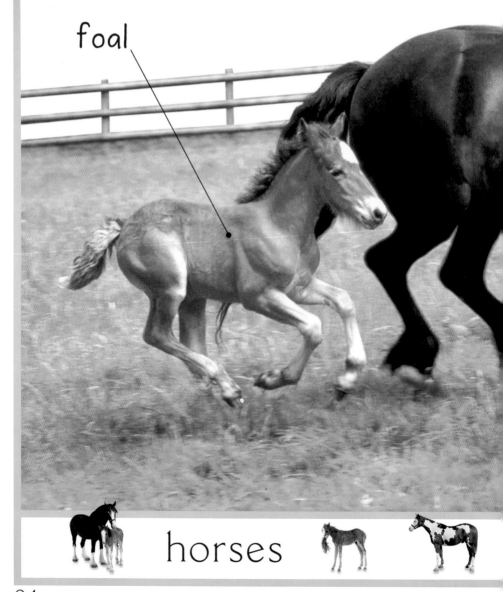

foal

horses

mane

ponies

Here are two ponies coming to see you.

pony

Here is a cat
curled up
with her kitten.

kitten

cats

hay

ear

Come and see us again soon!

Moo!

Which animals

Neigh!

do you like best?

Picture word list

chicken
page 6

turkey
page 8

pig
page 10

cow
page 12

dog
page 14

sheep
page 16

goat
page 18

duck
page 20

goose
page 22

horse
page 24

pony
page 26

cat
page 28